On Retirement

On Retirement

75 POEMS

EDITED BY

Robin Chapman

& Judith Strasser

UNIVERSITY OF IOWA PRESS

IOWA CITY

University of Iowa Press, Iowa City 52242
www.uiowapress.org
Copyright © 2007 by the University of Iowa Press
All rights reserved
Printed in the United States of America
Design by Sara T. Sauers

The University of Iowa Press is a member
of Green Press Initiative and is committed
to preserving natural resources.

Printed on acid-free paper

LCCN: 2006932732
ISBN-10: 1-58729-527-X
ISBN-13: 978-1-58729-527-0

07 08 09 10 11 P 5 4 3 2 1

Contents

Introduction

WE ARE KNOWN as the women who walk with lattés. Every Tuesday and Thursday for the past six years—since we retired from our jobs as professor (Robin) and radio producer (Judith)—we have started the morning with an hour-long walk that begins at one of our houses and takes us, first, to the closest coffee shop.

We've walked with umbrellas in rainstorms, savored the early cool of beastly summer days, and bundled up in long johns and face masks when the temperature stayed below zero. But, though the weather shifts with the seasons, our conversations circle the same themes. We talk about poetry, which is how we first came to know each other. We commiserate about rejection slips, celebrate acceptances, and discuss ideas for Robin's poems about the science of chaos and for student workshops that Judith leads. And we share news of our grown sons (we each have two), all of them living elsewhere; depending on the day, we fret or brag—as only two mothers can. But mostly we've helped each other step over the threshold of retirement into the uncertainty of changing identities, the challenges of illness and new relationships, and the joys of creating new lives for ourselves.

This collection grew out of these walks that began with our retirements. Both of us were born during World War II, just ahead of the baby boom. Judith retired at age fifty-five; Robin at fifty-seven. Statisticians say we can expect to live another twenty to thirty years; at least another whole quarter of our lives. And we are far from unique. Nearly eighty million Americans will reach retirement age in the next ten years, and will face—as we have—the unnerving question, What next? One morning as we walked, cardboard cups in our mittened hands, it occurred to us: some of those people are poets! They must be writing about this! And many more are lovers of poetry. What if we collected poems about retirement—and beyond? What if we edited an anthology? Would it help us all discover how to live the rest of our lives?

Because we started out as relatively young retirees, we rejoice in the "up" side of the fourth quarter: time to do what we really want to do, whether it be traveling the world, learning to play the cello, or falling in love again. But as we read through hundreds of poems—and as we ourselves grew older, and as one of us coped with a potentially fatal illness—we came to understand that in our retirement years, we all face losses as well as joys. As Doug Anderson notes in the first poem in this volume, "Death's a street away / walking parallel and at my pace. He gets a nod." But only a nod. We still have our lives to live!

People's experience of retirement follows a developmental arc that is reflected in the poems in this volume. First comes anticipation, as one imagines oneself older, joining the woman a decade ahead, as Lucille Clifton anticipates in her poem "climbing"; the "old guys" that haunt Wesley McNair; the midday shoppers in the hardware store of Robert Pinsky's poem.

Then as the actual day of retirement approaches, transition looms. The soon-to-be-retired worker reviews years on the job, often in the same office or classroom, as Jeri McCormick's "Bureaucrat" does; then says goodbye, like the "man overbored" klipschutz imagines, to the people and routines that have structured one's life.

In the days and months that follow, every retiree embarks on the delights and challenges of making a new life, deciding what to do with what their envious colleagues (and poet Roger Pfingston) call "all that time." Molly Peacock takes up drawing, Bill Brown turns his attention to the kingfisher in October, Meg Barden contemplates travel at age eighty. Gerald Stern celebrates a night at home in the company of music and Alvaros de Campos's poetry in "This Was a Wonderful Night." Like all of these poets—like us—Thomas Centolella welcomes "Some Little Happiness."

Three concerns loom large in the new life—and in these poems: aging and its inevitable effects on the body; generational connections to parents, children, and grandchildren; and the continuing satisfactions, losses, and renewals of love. With Susan Elbe, we discover that the "flesh that once loosened" our young selves now "limits" us. Chana Bloch laments the loss of words in "The Sixth Age." Self-assured and famous parents like Carolyn Kizer and Alicia Ostriker become the responsibilities of their "enormous children." Ronald Pies's neurology professor claims as his offspring "a thousand children / armed with reflex hammers / and soldier's heart." Rebecca Parfitt welcomes her granddaughter, seen in an ultrasound image;

Donna Wahlert takes heart from the visit of her three-year-old grandson. We hear the "tidal laughter" of the couple in Philip Booth's poem "Pairs" and—with poets Charles Cantrell, R. Virgil Ellis, and Alberto Ríos—reflect on enduring marriages. But we know, too, that relationships change: retired husbands, like the one in Marcia Denius's poem, suddenly take over the cooking and interior design. And Edith Nash notes that "only 52 years later" her husband finally likes the rye toast and poached eggs she serves for breakfast.

The poets gathered in this volume range in age from their fifties through their eighties. They include men and women from a variety of ethnic and racial backgrounds; residents of several continents, country acres, small towns, and big city apartments. We tried to gather a diverse group, but as we read and collected poems for this volume, we realized that many of our poets were teachers. Like us, the writers who appear in these pages are privileged: they've been able to set aside money for their later years; to leave their jobs and turn to something new. These poems don't speak for those who can't retire; or for the many retirees who—out of either financial need or curiosity—take up a new job rather than stop working. Nor do the poems speak for the adventurers and volunteers too busy to write as they explore new worlds.

Among our own friends, a chemical engineer has moved on to the Peace Corps, a clinical instructor in speech pathology has become a co-op supermarket clerk, a computer systems analyst has turned to tutoring first-grade readers. Too few of our poems note the wide range of unpaid jobs that retirees are taking up: volunteering for Red Cross disaster teams and homeless shelters, delivering Meals on Wheels, ushering for concerts and plays. Finally, we ask ourselves, what does "retirement" mean to writers who continue to turn out poems and stories until the day they die? As John Brandi suggests, some people love their work so much they don't think of it as a job. Does that mean they can't retire?

Perhaps the most difficult part of editing this volume has been finding a balance between the pleasures of retirement, the indignities of aging, and death itself. However much we savor our new lives, retirement also represents loss: loss of our old identity, of our daily interaction with colleagues, of youth. We have been both surprised and consoled by the plain-spoken and often humorous approach many poets take to these losses. Hayden Carruth chastised us when we asked permission to reprint a poem that captured the delights of retirement, "Where the hell have you been living, my dears, that you don't know old age is the greatest bummer and pisser of all times and places, without comparison or exception? Ask anyone over eighty."

We are still far from eighty. But we have taken heart from the words of Hayden Carruth and the other poets in this volume. No one poem can map the future. Still, taken together, these poems explore the rocky but beautiful territory of retirement, and beyond. They've helped us on our journeys through the transition from "working stiffs" to "retired seniors": we've become accepting enough of our new status to sign up for an Elderhostel (Judith) and a Golden Age Passport for the National Parks (Robin). We're confident that the poems will help you, too. So order up a latté, brew yourself a cup of tea, or pour yourself a glass of wine or water, and enjoy!

On Retirement

DOUG ANDERSON

Sixty-One

Fifty was poignant, heavy pear
departs the tree and the poem
a sigh between branch and mulch.
But no more. Another decade,
I'm all song and scruff,
the mind's hot wire threading joint to joint.
I'll tell you straight out what I think,
no sweetener. Nor has Aphrodite left me
collapsed in a stairwell
and don't you father-flirt me, girl.
This morning the world unbelts her robe,
rose fleshed and randy.
I like the rats that skitter
under the subway's hot rails.
The little black dog
who's afraid of no one,
not even the dope dealer's pitbulls.
Montaigne said sickness
is God's way of weaning us from life
but I don't think yet. I like the way
soul clings to gristle like a newspaper
wrapped around a light pole in a storm.
Death's a street away
walking parallel and at my pace. He gets a nod.

Who Is Not a Child

translated by Robin Fulton

One day in my seventieth year on earth
when I tried to remember what it felt like
to be a newcomer in the world and on my own
to find its seven and seventy entrances

I was helped by a professor emeritus,
master of seven languages,
who stood in the hallway on the verge of tears
trying to get his hand into the arm of his coat.

Insisting on doing it himself.

And who of us is not a child
and who is not a professor?

Eliseo's Cabin, Taos Pueblo

Yellow alfalfa banks the rutted lane
that winds in under the bedstead gate
latched with loops of baling wire.
Horseskulls bleach on fenceposts
running down through sagebrush
to the cabin snug by the sandy creek.
Pieces of plows hang from the cedars
along with barn hinges, tractor chains,
and a rusted-out kettle. A buffalo hide
drapes a lodge pole wedged in willows.
The cabin's covered in sweetpea vines,
blossoms tumbling out bees.
Eliseo has set his cot outside
near an iron pot brimming peonies.

Lying alone at night, watching
stars shake, hearing the creek talk,
he remembers before there was a camp
and his father would come here to watch
thunderheads collapse on the prairie
and drag sweeps of rain across arroyos.
Worried about the old man sleeping on the ground
he sawed planks and hauled them up by buckboard
rocking to the meadow on wheels that smelled of sage.

Now old himself he comes to his cabin
to heat chili and bread on the wood stove
to sleep by the creek or sit by a spruce
whittling birds for grandchildren.
In the dark, he hears his ponies graze
across the fern-crowded creek
where fireflies flare like memories
and his father and grandchildren's voices
rise from the cold traveling water.

3

Reaching Eighty

Why don't I want to
meander in Morocco markets
or stroll down the Ramblas in Barcelona,
listening for a rooster, watching the caged canaries?
Neither do I long for the mermaid
in Copenhagen Harbor.
It doesn't matter that I missed the Matterhorn
and never sailed the Volga.

Perhaps you could persuade me to
join the Zapatistas in Chiapas,
or to transport bicycles to Havana.
I might help immigrants from Cambodia
or fight for peace in Zimbabwe.

For now, I watch the people going past my window:
a plump baby pushed in a stroller
by his slim, hurried mother in a blue hat;
a white-haired couple
striding together without a limp or a pause.
At 8 A.M. the Middle School students hurry past
wearing faded jeans and backpacks.
While I await the dark-haired mail lady
moving gracefully
despite the heavy load on her shoulder,
bringing me words from all the world.

Bamboo

Off a back street courtyard in Jinan, a gray
hall flowers with bright brush paintings
by elderly men and women who gather
to meet us. They wear old Mao suits
as if they have slept in them for years.
They sit shyly while their leader demonstrates
how to paint bamboo on silk.
       But we are tired.
We have seen too much bamboo already.
During the question period we hardly ask
our counterparts anything. We walk around
smiling at the walls, wondering what these people
did before they got old. Worked in the silk mills,
picked soybeans? One small woman shuffles
up to me and points out her painting above us,
a blood-red peony. She tells me she speaks
a little English. I look for a suitable
question to give her.
     "What did you do
before you retired?" She bows her head as if
receiving a blessing, answers, "For China
throughout seven provinces I designed
railroad stations. Also my design,
this next picture of bamboo."

Unwise Purchases

They sit around in the house
Not doing much of anything: the boxed set
Of the complete works of Verdi, unopened.
The complete Proust, unread.
The French cut silk shirts
Which hang like expensive ghosts in the closet,
And make me look exactly
Like the kind of middle-aged man
Who would wear a French cut silk shirt.

The reflector telescope I thought would unlock
The mysteries of the heavens
But which I used only once or twice,
And which now stares disconsolately at the ceiling
When it could be examining the Crab Nebula.

The 30-day course in Spanish,
Whose text I barely opened,
Whose dozen cassette tapes remain unplayed,
Save for Tape One, where I never learned
Whether the suave American,
Conversing with a sultry-sounding desk clerk
At a Spanish hotel about the possibility
Of obtaining a room,
Actually managed to check in. I like to think
That one thing led to another between them
And that by Tape Six or so
They're happily married
And raising a bilingual child in Seville or Terre Haute.

But I'll never know.

Suddenly I realize
I have constructed the perfect home
For a sexy, Spanish-speaking astronomer
Who reads Proust while listening to Italian arias,
And I wonder if somewhere in this teeming city
There lives a woman with, say,
A fencing foil gathering dust in the corner
Near her unused easel, a rainbow
Of oil paints drying in their tubes
On the table where the violin lies entombed
In the permanent darkness of its locked case
Next to the dusty chess set,

A woman who has always dreamed of becoming
The kind of woman the man I've dreamed of becoming
Has always dreamed of meeting,

And while the two of them discuss star clusters
And Cézanne, while they fence delicately
In Castilian Spanish to the strains of *Rigoletto*,

She and I will stand in the steamy kitchen,
Fixing up a little risotto,
Enjoying a modest cabernet
While talking over a day so ordinary
As to seem miraculous.

CHANA BLOCH

The Sixth Age

Words slip from me lately like cups and saucers
from soapy hands.
I grope for the names of things
that are governed, like me, by the laws
of slippage and breakage.

I am like a child
left behind by the fast-talking grownups.
Like a tourist trapped in the blind alleys
of a foreign language.

How will I see my way from here to anywhere
without my words?

I slam up and down the stairs of the house:
Where are my glasses hiding?
Rimless plastic invisible as the sky.
I need glasses to find them.

I need the words that are left
to go on searching for the ones I've lost

the way the blind man I loved once
found me,
first with his fingertips,
then with the whole of his hand.

PHILIP BOOTH ✒

Pairs

Years now, good days
more than half the year,

they row late afternoons
out through the harbor

to the bell, a couple
with gray hair, an old

green rowboat. Given sun,
their four oars, stroke

by stroke, glint wet,
so far away that even

in light air their
upwind voices barely

carry. No words translate
to us on shore, more

than a mile from where
they pull and feather.

All we hear is how,
like sea-ducks, they

seem constantly to
murmur. And even

after summer's gone,
as they row out or

home, now and again
we hear, we cannot help

but hear, their years
of tidal laughter.

JONATHAN BRACKER

Wait-Time Is Currently about Twelve Minutes

God, I realize you screen all calls. A busy Person
Often walking a good-natured weimaraner in our neighborhood park,
Lobbing her a chartreuse tennis ball with the newly invented ball-tosser,
Cell-phoning Gabriel your whereabouts, smoking a clove cigarette,
You are forever occupied.

Were we to pass on magnolia-shaded sidewalk
I would quickly, appreciatively glance, expecting no Hello.
Now I request your e-mail address, wanting to believe that you are there.
To be used only in an emergency. Please send it;
You know mine.

I was not upset when you got one bicep tied with a blue tattoo band
And had a nostril pierced for that simple gold ring,
Only at first a little surprised. More sympathetic now,
I see you trying to look young
And keeping pace with your offsprings' creations.

Restless in retirement, like me you walk through fears
And are willing to risk new things;
I respect you for being no fogey.
I swear I would use it only in an emergency—
Not merely in moments of terror.

thinking of retirement
he realizes
he never had a job

Waking

I wake each morning and read the window for weather,
as drops of condensation run down the pane
like mist on magnolia. Soft morning illuminates
the bedroom, and even early birds mute their songs.

How slow time wakes when work is forgotten,
and obligations drift out the kitchen window
like the scent of coffee. September has come and gone
with little to say except everything that lives past summer

doesn't die. October isn't a preface to winter,
but a sky-blue month when rain turns cold,
clouds float high and lonely, and our little star makes
broken shadows of leaves drifting across the river.

Today a kingfisher rattles his journey through the valley,
and two crows preen first light into morning.
This is how I learn to say my name again, since waking
isn't a metaphor, and time means more than money.

Retirement Matters

What mattered: bulging wallet,
like cabbages in our garden.
What mattered: love on sweaty
nights, lemonade, TV . . . Now, TV
flattens thin plots thinner, so I drift
into a magazine article, which tries
to explain lust. What matters is you
as we hold each other between
tragedies: someone on a jet
lights a fuse in his sock.
Someone down the block
knocks his daughter's teeth loose. . . .

What matters: you lean toward your
asters while I wander a railroad track—
plum, cherry, hawthorn past barbed wire—
blossomed perfume hovering
beneath the moon. Sometimes I brush
against pine needles or red sumac,
even picture myself as a flying squirrel
or a jack-hammering woodpecker.

Sometimes an owl or a hawk
cracks a limb overhead. What cracks
in the heart is never stocks or bonds
but what to say: to say it right, rhythm
and tone exact—same as the top wire
of our fence, still shiny after years,
where you drop popcorn and bread crusts
near the feeder for starlings and blue jays
while goldfinch and warblers wait, and we,
behind the door's window, point and hold.

HAYDEN CARRUTH 🪶

At Seventy-Five
Rereading an Old Book

My prayers have been answered, if they were prayers. I live.
I'm alive, and even in rather good health, I believe.
If I'd quit smoking I might live to be a hundred.
Truly this is astonishing, after the poverty and pain,
The suffering. Who would have thought that petty
Endurance could achieve so much?
                                        And prayers—
Were they prayers? Always I was adamant
In my irreligion, and had good reason to be.
Yet prayer is not, I see in old age now,
A matter of doctrine or discipline, but rather
A movement of the natural human mind
Bereft of its place among the animals, the other
Animals. I prayed. Then on paper I wrote
Some of the words I said, which are these poems.

In the Pinecrest Rest Home

Mrs. P doesn't know her husband,
Mr. P doesn't know his wife,
but there they sit in the morning sun
waiting to be noticed.
Inwardness is not what God wants
so she adjusts her chair
and moves to where he sits looking at
the center of the rose—examining it for origins.
They introduce themselves, each day,
shy at first, careful so as not to harm.
Leisure and light favor them.
They both like cats.
Both agree it doesn't mean
that's all there is to value. Oh no—
And so the conversation grows. He
plucks, from time to time, some petals—
pulls them off. Infidelity is absence
of desire. This, unspoken, but they seem
to know to stay away
from others walking by. The ground shifts
beneath their feet when names are called. It scares them.
Giving up a fixed view, they think of each other at
night while lying on their separate beds. They
wonder about their strange talks, having the same memories.

THOMAS CENTOLELLA

Some Little Happiness

knows our names
and where we live
and sets out to meet us halfway.

It arrives humming,
an enchantment of tones
we have never heard
and don't want to let go,
because we know
they will never be heard again.

Some little happiness lives
in our eyes, in our skin,
leaves a trace in the lines
around our tired mouths.

Some little happiness.

We don't have to deserve it,
we don't have to expect it,
we don't even have to admit
how much we need it,

and some little happiness
will rest its hand on our hands,
will tell us, Take me,
I won't be here that long,
and neither will you.

It's okay, whispers
some little happiness,
trust me.

And we do.

The Inspector of Snowstorms

Retiring, I look for a new occupation, want
to appoint myself, like Thoreau, an inspector
of weather, but there's so much else to do—
bicycle trails to walk or ride, garlic mustard
to pull, the crane count to make in the marsh,
the prairie to burn and sow; or, slower still,
the woods to walk about, ears tuning in
the stations of wood duck and vireo, oriole
and crow, or the eye finding the prisms
of morning beaded on wild geranium leaves,
light brushed by the mouse ears of oak
overhead, each day new in the marsh, each evening
visiting a friend like Emerson or Alcott,
each night the heart wandering through words
like the eye through the spinning stars of summer,
or the winter veils of never-the-same snowflakes
weighting the stripped trees and underbrush.

God and Goddess

They hang out together in late middle age.
They're still busy but they're looking forward to retirement.

Which they will spend relaxing on a screen porch,
live oak, azalea, and palmettos shading the birdbath on the back lawn.
He'll go fishing.
She'll look through the family photo albums.

Here are pictures of the children:

> those who did well,
> those who did good,
>
> those who thought they could do better
> than the old man
> and were surprised
> when they returned from far off
> to discover that their hearts had burned down
> and they had to rebuild.

climbing

a woman precedes me up the long rope,
her dangling braids the color of rain.
maybe i should have had braids.
maybe i should have kept the body i started,
slim and possible as a boy's bone.
maybe i should have wanted less.
maybe i should have ignored the bowl in me
burning to be filled.
maybe i should have wanted less.
the woman passes the notch in the rope
marked Sixty. i rise toward it, struggling,
hand over hungry hand.

A Visitation

We sit at our kitchen table,
uncomfortable with so much room.
I hear echoes of laughter and crying
but all I see is shadows
and an old man
in whom I am mirrored.

We compete in the Grandparent Olympiad,
timing how long each baby
allowed us to coo on the telephone.
We love our quiet routine,
and even know where the Scotch tape
and magic marker are.

Until one day they all arrive
tumbling from planes, jumping from cars,
bursting through the door, just as they
tumbled and burst forth from me
with innocent violent eagerness,
sure of their welcome.

The house rings with shouts of merriment and outrage.
Meals are feasts and food fights.
We walk carefully, head down, lest we trip
over a toy that has been left
carelessly lying around
in territorial assertion.

We wake to small children
crawling over us,
sticking fingers into our mouths and eyes.
The oldest announces, "We is hungry and we is thirsty."
We reach for a fresh diaper
thoughtfully left in a stack on our bed table.

Just as we cannot bear the cacophony
another minute, they pack
their suitcases, tuck the toys back
in the attic.
Our children turn into adult strangers
holding babies, who wave good-bye.

Suddenly, we feel old.

RUTH DAIGON 🖎

To the Woman Who Left Her Old Age to Someone Older than She Will Ever Be

On the day I finally
outlive your days, I'll
wake to leaf fire
sunlight
peeling eucalyptus
and room enough to drown in.

But I'll still float above your kitchen-talk
in rooms of broken English.
What you wouldn't give
to have that dream again
daughters with sweet heft of breasts
sons on long stems of bones.

Isadora danced naked on the sand
but you patrolled the shore
trapped in dailyness
chafing your bunions on the beach
rushing to see
if one of us had drowned.

What full-time work it was
for you to live
days sucked into sinks
full of dishes
nights spent ironing
every stroke a small act of love.

California shines and shines.
Summer builds earthworks all year round.
Sun glows electric.
I draw long, even breaths for you
turn and breathe and make such
simple crossings back again.

Rest Cure

Ernie sleeps day and night
He is taking his post-vacation
rest from obeying Velma's
warnings on road hazards
potholes patrol cars pedestrians
swatting mosquitos
inspecting her for ticks
swimming sailing
trailering lifting
kayaks to the water
Velma from the kayak
heavy with fatigue
shopping grilling
negotiating craft show
traffic jams
eating fried fish fried dough
not the boneless skinless
fat free food from home
sitting in the shade
waiting while Velma visits
27 antique shops in three days
Ernie's patience has worn him out

On His Early Retirement

I arrive home at the end of the day
to the smell of burnt toast,
overlaid with fresh spritzes of floral-scent spray.

He's in the kitchen singing off-key,
surrounded by pots and pans, and cabinet doors
open wide. I bite my tongue as I see
the gallon or two of stew he's concocted
boil onto the burner out of the crock—
he's discovered he loves to cook!

He asks how my day went,
stops the wooden spoon's stirring, and listens . . .
he listens! . . . to my offhand reply,
hoping to note an event in my daily routine
that next time he too could partake in—
he now wants to do things with me!

So we're off to the store for the groceries he needs
to finish the stew—he scours the shelves,
taking his time to consider each item,
reading labels, pinching the veggies and fruit,
and he wants help in deciding between green
or red peppers—he asks my advice!

Back at home, I go to set the table for supper
in what always has been the room we dine in,
but find it's not anymore: it's turned into his office—
he's discovered interior design!

What's more, he tells me his plans for tomorrow
include painting the fridge black—
just like the ones he's seen in the 'zines

I used to read when I had the time.
He assures me I'll agree with the statement it makes:
Drop-dead dramatic, yet toney!

I'm thinking, thank God for my job,
although he's always asking when I'll be back
as I'm asking myself when will he leave?
And . . . is this what it's like, having a wife?

MARY L. DOWNS

Flu Clinic at the Retirement Center

Gathered like restless sheep
in a strange holding pen
Medicare cards in hand
we wait to be called
to the Community Room
turned dispensary

Resident volunteers record
names, addresses, ages
shepherd us in line
summon the lost and tardy
check us off as we enter
the injection site   where

a nurse tallies Medicare numbers
mentions chicken feathers and eggs
questions prior reactions
Ignoring someone's cheeky remarks
we offer bared upper left limbs
meek as lambs   to a second nurse

who administers the vaccine
applies kiddie band-aids
With a "nothing to it" attitude
we roll down long sleeves
pull on sweaters and file out
grateful for a year's protection

Do we think we won't get sick?
Bah!   Not by a long shot

The Carpenter's Song

for Ted Porter

When I'm no longer young
let me be able to make wine
from chokecherries and care enough
to let it age. And when friends come
let them sip it
on a torn-out car seat under a tree.
And let my house smell of books
and pipe smoke, and let its disarray
be the luxury of a man
who makes cabinets.
And after it gets dark
let's move to the room
where the squeeze-box is, sing songs
and talk of Iceland by freighter,
Newfoundland on a whim, all the arrivals
one doesn't plan.
And let the evidence be deep
in my voice, the lines of my face.
And let me call this: style.

Let me rebuild then the lighthouse
my father rebuilt years ago,
and let me know the history
of old houses haunted by rats
and shadows, good people
and bad, and when asked
let me sense what can be redeemed
and what can't.
And yes, let me be able to say
I'm a builder of houses, a man
who works slow and knows
how hard it is

to get the inside just right.
And let my metaphors grow
from that, something lived stretching out
trying to make contact
with something else.
And let me call this: my work.

And when I'm no longer young
let there be poets in my life,
their words aftertastes on the tongue,
and let me speak those words like a man
who has heard a spar snap on a ship,
who has been lost once or twice
and come back.
And let me declare
I've been a lover of women
without declaring it, and feel
I've treated them better than wood,
knowing I've been a husband of wood,
have cared for it with my own hands.
And let my hands be thick
badges of power
rarely used, my fist an inner fist
the size of a heart,
and let this be visible to men.
And let the old deaf dog
sense me coming a long way off,
ready to forgive anything I've done—
and let me call all this: some goddamn luck.

SUSAN ELBE

Brooding over the Body

We are not our bodies, I tell my friend
because we're middle-aged,
chafing at its insolent betrayal—

one day, desire
quickening the pulse
like moths skittering to light,

the next,
you bend to tie your shoes
and can't breathe,
heart
slapping at your windpipe
like a trout trapped in a creel.

You'd swear some nights
a raven hunches in your ribcage
nipping nerve ends,
scratching at your gullet.

In its harsh and crooked way,
it calls you
from dream-freighted sleep
to walk the floor and wonder
how this scavenger got in.

I tell her *we are spirit, will,*
the sum of soul and wit.

Yet this morning at the mirror,
looking at the slack moon-
crescents of my breasts,
the widening span of hips
and thickening waist,

I wondered at how quickly
the body pulls us down, heavy
with its own warm brine and tides.

No matter that the girl in me
still wants to sprint
up stairs, love till dawn,
and glut on cheese and cream.

This flesh that loosened me
limits me.

In the too-bright bathroom light,
I splay my starfish hands,

the rambling veins now
less like fine-penned blueprints
and more like bare-branched trees.

Still, my wrists, still
slender as a girl's.

Heading towards Forty

years of marriage, that many years of age
having slid by a generation ago. It's slippery
still. We negotiate the curves each day throws.
You can't mix too many metaphors trying to nail
what holds us together. Don't be too precise
or you might knock out a hidden strut and the
whole shay will come apart. Instead pin a rose
for how we both let nasty particulars slide.
Given this much time I have just about learned
how to pick up my socks. You have almost
(though of course not quite) gotten the knack
of turning out lights. If we can't imagine
what holds other couples together think of
what they must think of us. What we overlook
teeters against what we admire. What a joke
to think gramps and gran are set in their ways
with never a leaping desire. Sometimes we make
love as good as we ever did. It wasn't easy learning
to live with my smolder. It's been no lark for you
to watch me finger the remote, tubing out
instead of coming to bed. Sometimes we read
together there, with the small light and the time
sliding by. It's getting late, we should get to sleep.
In the dark we hold hands, then turn aside.
How much promise there is in compromise.

DIANE GLANCY

No Clomping Straightforward Narrative
There Is an Abstraction in Aging Only Abstraction Can Relay

A ball of twine in a drawer.
A wall made of field stones.
The stripes of a tiger melon.
A bosc pear.
The tundra.
The flight of an Arctic tern.

SAM HAMILL

The Orchid Flower

Just as I wonder
whether it's going to die,
the orchid blossoms

and I can't explain why it
moves my heart, why such pleasure

comes from one small bud
on a long spindly stem, one
blood red gold flower

opening at mid-summer,
tiny, perfect in its hour.

Even to a white-
haired craggy poet, it's
purely erotic,

pistil and stamen, pollen,
dew of the world, a spoonful

of earth, and water.
Erotic because there's death
at the heart of birth,

drama in those old sunrise
prisms in wet cedar boughs,

deepest mystery
in washing evening dishes
or teasing my wife,

who grows, yes, more beautiful
because one of us will die.

JIM HANLEN

Retirement

No more kids in the last row,
Only mountains to talk to.

They do pay attention
And every morning they're on time.

Now there are ferns and stones,
Kids, the noise and bells, a memory.

When I dip my finger in the creek
I write the clearest words.

And my dreams,
A little red fish every night.

The Work Place

So what is this intimacy
not of flesh,
not of smell or touch
or texture,
not of deeply personal
exchanges;
more often than not
the casual, the obvious,
the what-is-necessary,
the daily.
What have we become
together
over the years in this room
that is different
from what we've become
with other people?
What binds us?
Have we simply become
habits for each other?
And is love really
after all
an accumulation of
shared habits?
What makes a departure
so fateful?
How much of me
will you take away
when you go?
I do not know.
I only ask.
What have we
become together
in this room?

Last Minute Instructions

Now that I'm gone, my dearest,
I wish you the very best.
Our lawyer will do all the legal work,
don't let it trouble your head.
Take my clothes to the Goodwill store,
they'll look great on another dude.
Choose the car you like the best,
take the other to Joe for sale.
Oh, and keep a bottle of Pabst in the fridge
in memory of me.

Keep up with your friends,
you're much too young to be alone.
And if, as time passes quietly by,
you meet a man whose vibes match yours,
after you've taken time to be rightly sure,
give him the Pabst to drink.

Mansion of Happiness

People stand in front of a large white house giving
things away. June light floods the windows and occasionally
they look up as toward a familiar song. They stand on
the slow green hill of their lives. The air smells with rain
and the flowers are in want of their hands. They give
things away because their bodies are tired. Distant, a jet strays,
its tiny silver lozenge an impossible word. A woman says
"I remember Will" and a slight wind moves through the trees. Belief
is this language pulling them together, holding them
apart. The words need them so. Someone passes cookies
around on a silver tray. There are chairs everywhere
but no one is sitting down. How important it is to love
what is gone. Mary says "my son" and the word is handled
—clean and simple—like an egg peeled of its shell. Everywhere people
are whispering "I want you to have . . . " Detached from everything
they are open to all. Love's pollen flies. Dandelions spill
bright coins on the lawn. Shadows stretch out long. Trees pool
against sky, the pale joinery of clouds. A bird sings *how*
long, how long, while a boy listening to his Walkman, walks
down the road. Everyone turns and smiles. They watch him
watch the world. Soon they will go inside before the house is gone.

RUTH HARRIET JACOBS 🖋

Assorted Hobbies

Retired, he goes frequently
to free financial seminars
that bribe with lunch or dinner
sometimes he invites a woman friend
making for a cheap date

She takes stacks of paper napkins
plastic spoons, sugar packets
from self-serve restaurants
and extra supermarket bags
overflow her cabinets

Every single Saturday
they look at houses for sale
titillating owners and agents
as they inspect every inch
that they will never buy

Ham and the Moon

Sit down
and I'll feed you.
Ladle up a bowl of lentil soup,
a little ocean
full of sun and warmth.
Add a salad made of peppers
hot as fallen stars,
avocados, olives,
just a touch of lemon juice
and garlic.

I am not a world class cook
but for you, my friend,
I'll stay up all night
sweating in my kitchen
to bring the cuisine
of eleven nations
to your plate by morning.
You are sick
and you will die,
the doctors say,
but I refuse to let it be
from starvation.

So here, straight from the South,
green beans cooked all day
and my finest crabcakes,
each fork, each taste
a reason to keep living.
For dessert, cherries
so ripe they whisper
carpe diem
or would if cherries

knew much Latin.
After such a dinner,
we can wipe our mouths
clean of crumbs
and of regret.

Because I do not kid myself.
I know the future,
that iron door,
will be there waiting
no matter what
I have baking in the oven.
But in the meantime,
there are ears of sweet corn
and a mother lode of mussels
it is clear God made
especially for steaming.
Take a seat at my table,
I'll cook them up for you.

Parents' Pantoum

for Maxine Kumin

Where did these enormous children come from,
More ladylike than we have ever been?
Some of ours look older than we feel.
How did they appear in their long dresses

More ladylike than we have ever been?
But they moan about their aging more than we do,
In their fragile heels and long black dresses.
Then say they admire our youthful spontaneity.

They moan about their aging more than we do,
A somber group—why don't they brighten up?
Though they say they admire our youthful spontaneity
They beg us to be dignified like them

As they ignore our pleas to brighten up.
Someday perhaps we'll capture their attention,
Then we won't try to be dignified like them
Nor they to be so gently patronizing.

Someday perhaps we'll capture their attention.
Don't they know that we're supposed to be the stars?
Instead they are so gently patronizing.
It makes us feel like children—second-childish?

Perhaps we're too accustomed to be stars,
The famous flowers glowing in the garden,
So now we pout like children. Second-childish?
Quaint fragments of forgotten history?

Our daughters stroll together in the garden,
Chatting of news we've chosen to ignore,
Pausing to toss us morsels of their history,
Not questions to which only we know answers.

Eyes closed to news we've chosen to ignore,
We'd rather excavate old memories,
Disdaining age, ignoring pain, avoiding mirrors.
Why do they never listen to our stories?

Because they hate to excavate old memories
They don't believe our stories have an end.
They don't ask questions because they dread the answers.
They don't see that we've become their mirrors,

We offspring of our enormous children.

Office

i

Spy with me
on this train going nowhere,
while the ice age advances
without pity.

Watch me watching
the green numbers dancing,
their thin paper tresses
curling to the floor.

See my eyes light up
when I put somebody on hold.

ii

The lunchroom meets the lunch truck
with the secret handshake
in a noonal landscape of burrito wrappers
and apple cores.

iii

These crisply cornered walls,
these tinted windows looking out
on tinted windows looking out from other
crisply cornered walls—

no wonder
I keep losing
my desk.

iv

Twoish. Slowish.
Man overbored! Man overbored!
Quick someone, toss him a life-saver,
or maybe a candy bar.

v

I am an alien in the heart of matter—

working harder and harder falling further behind.
Furthermore, I'm losing weight and getting fatter!

Well, it's all paying off
(better phone Wife):

On the first I go on deficit sharing . . .

vi

Stand by, this is serious and
penultimate.
But it's not as if there's
nowhere else to go.

Or is there? Is this the end of the line?
Are those ceiling lights the conductor's
face?

Do we really go home at night? How can we be
sure?

Applesauce

I liked how the starry blue lid
of that saucepan lifted and puffed,
then settled back on a thin
hotpad of steam, and the way
her kitchen filled with the warm,
wet breath of apples, as if all
the apples were talking at once,
as if they'd come cold and sour
from chores in the orchard,
and were trying to shoulder in
close to the fire. She was too busy
to put in her two cents' worth
talking to apples. Squeezing
her dentures with wrinkly lips,
she had to jingle and stack
the bright brass coins of the lids
and thoughtfully count out
the red rubber rings, then hold
each jar, to see if it was clean,
to a window that looked out
through her back yard into Iowa.
And with every third or fourth jar
she wiped steam from her glasses,
using the hem of her apron,
printed with tiny red sailboats
that dipped along with leaf-green
banners snapping, under puffs
of pale applesauce clouds
scented with cinnamon and cloves,
the only boats under sail
for at least two thousand miles.

ELLEN KORT

One by One

She learned to rearrange her life
as if each turning day was a piece
of furniture   She learned to make things fit
pushing a chair closer to an open door
next to a window   taking the drapes down
inviting more light   She lived alone now
and liked it   her red garden boots
by the front door   a bag of bird seed   large
and comforting in the corner of the kitchen
a daily ritual she could count on

One day she took her mother's white bowl
from the top shelf of the cupboard   placed it
in the middle of the kitchen table and filled it
with clear glass marbles   Each morning
she chose one   held it in her hand   carried it
in her pocket where she could thumb
its warm smoothness   and when she was ready
she planted it in her garden
or threw it in the river   put it in a bird's
empty nest or buried it behind the garage
Sometimes she carried one into town
and left it for a child to find   or dropped it
in the loose-change cup at the gas station

She tried to give what she was doing a name
but nothing seemed to fit   It had nothing
to do with what her heart depended on
or how she might live the rest of her life
She simply liked the ceremony of each small
universe in the palm of her hand   the daily
practice   the momentary kindness of letting go

Women and Horses

After Auschwitz, to write a poem is barbaric.
—Theodor Adorno

After Auschwitz: after ten of my father's kin—
the ones who stayed—starved, then were gassed in the camps.
After Vietnam, after Korea, Kuwait, Somalia, Haiti, Afghanistan.
After the Towers. This late in the life of our haplessly orbiting world
let us celebrate whatever scraps the muse, that naked child,
can pluck from the still-smoldering dumps.

If there's a lyre around, strike it! A body, stand back, give it air!
Let us have sparrows laying their eggs in bluebird boxes.
Let us have bluebirds insouciantly nesting elsewhere.
Lend us navel-bared teens, eyebrowed- and nose-ringed prodigies
crumbling breakfast bagels over dogeared and jelly-smeared texts.
Allow the ablebodied among us to have steamy sex.

Let there be fat old ladies in flowery tent dresses at bridge tables.
Howling babies in dirty diapers and babies serenely at rest.
War and detente will go on, detente and renewed tearings asunder,
we can never break free from the dark and degrading past.
Let us see life again, nevertheless, in the words of Isaac Babel
as a meadow over which women and horses wander.

Living Alone (III)

I said, the summer garden I planted
bears only leaves—leaves in abundance—
but no flowers.
And then the flowers,
      many colors and forms,
      subtle, mysterious,
came forth.

I said, the tree has no buds.
And then the leaves,
      shyly, sparse, as if reluctant,

in less than two days appeared,
and the tree, now,
      is flying on green wings.

What magic denial
shall my life utter
to bring itself forth?

SANDRA LINDOW

The Physicist's Warning
with apologies to Jenny Joseph

When I am old, I shall wear ultra-violet
and a red Doppler shift that doesn't go, and doesn't suit me.
And I shall spend my pension on large crystal lenses,
star flung champagne and small velvet purses
that remind me of black holes. I'll spend everything on shuttle tickets
then say we have no money for nuclear warheads.

I shall visit the Hubble Telescope if I am tired
and call press conferences with stories of alien encounters.
I'll make up for the studiousness of my youth
by writing science fictional bodice rippers and submitting
them as papers to academic conferences.
I'll go to the observatory in silk kimono and fuzzy slippers
and borrow a centrifuge to mix chocolate chip cookies.

I shall polish my hot flashes until they take on a brilliance
of their own. Sometimes I'll forget to eat; other times
I'll eat Blue Moon Ice Cream for a week until my elimination
becomes blue shifted, thereby disproving universal expansion.
I'll steal paper clips from others' file cabinets, hoard
laser pens, yellow pads, and colored stars in tiny boxes.
Sometimes I'll wear stars in my hair.

For now I shall wear sensible shoes that cushion my arches,
pay all my taxes, and forswear swearing in faculty meetings.
I'll set a good example for graduate students
by inviting alumni to dinner and reading long journal articles;
but maybe I ought to practice a bit now
so my colleagues are not so shocked and surprised
when ensconced in a fabric of ultra-violet, I rise
beyond realms of visible light and barriers of audible sound.

ARLENE L. MANDELL

All Dressed Up

A bit of gel to tame
my springy curls,
a clean T-shirt and shorts,
sandals and sun screen,
most days this is all
I need for the library,
hardware store or
farmers' market.

Switch to white slacks,
add earrings and a squirt
of green tea cologne
and I'm ready for
our indie film house
followed by a tasty meal
at bistro or barbecue joint.

Once I wore linen suits,
pantyhose, sling-back pumps
and makeup—foundation,
liner, blush, mascara—
so much time and money
to project that chic
public relations image.

Now retirement is my profession
and I'm out the door in ten minutes.

Almost Eighty

A white bird whiter
              than the white moon
flies up and over
              the parading apple trees
and you closer and closer
              to that dark gate
listen for death

hear only silence
imagine the glide of feathers
as a long pianissimo whir
arcing over the moon
and the white moon-glitter of leaves
an echo of marimbas

but now, clear, authoritative,
pitched low, coming from the shallows
real sound, frogs
in guttural staccato.
Why this waiting for death?
Maybe near
an exact time chosen

but under the moon
              aloft with the bird
grounded by frogs
part of the now
why care?

JERI MCCORMICK

Bureaucrat Tells How

Start with Monday
Enter some glass doors
Board the cube-cell
Shaft your way up
Greet the counter person
Dispense some smiles
Check your message bin
Empty your mail box
Hang up your coat

Walk to your cubicle
Say good morning
Say good morning
Say good morning
Sit in your padded chair
Spread out some papers
Become the idea somebody had
Turn on the computer
Write some memos

Look at the clock
Get some coffee
Make three phone calls
Attend a meeting
Check your message bin
Report to your boss
Listen to some jokes
Look at the clock
Post some mail
Eat some lunch

Read the paper
Check your message bin
Explain something to someone
Eavesdrop at the next cube
Ask someone to explain
Look at the clock
Get some coffee
Fill out some forms
Make three phone calls

Attend a training session
Check your message bin
Look at the clock
Turn off your computer
Tidy up your desk
Say goodnight
Say goodnight
Say goodnight
Put on your coat

Board the cube-cell
Shaft your way down
Exit the glass doors
Do this Tuesday
Do this Wednesday
Do this Thursday
Do this Friday
Do this 1,900 weeks
Say goodbye over cake
Go forth and see what's left

Old Guys

Driving beyond a turn in the mist
of a certain morning, you'll find them
beside a men-at-work sign,
standing around with their caps on
like penguins, all bellies and bills.
They'll be watching what the yellow truck
is doing and how. Old guys know trucks,
having spent days on their backs under them
or cars. You've seen the gray face
of the garage mechanic lying on his pallet, old
before his time, and the gray, as he turns
his wrench looking up through the smoke
of his cigarette, around the pupil
of his eye. This comes from concentrating
on things the rest of us refuse
to be bothered with, like the thickening
line of dirt in front of the janitor's
push broom as he goes down the hall, or the same
ten eyelets inspector number four checks
on the shoe, or the box after box
the newspaper man brings to a stop
in the morning dark outside the window
of his car. Becoming expert in such details
is what has made the retired old guy
behind the shopping cart at the discount store
appear so lost. Beside him his large wife,
who's come through poverty and starvation
of feeling, hungry for promises of more
for less, knows just where she is,
and where and who she is sitting by his side
a year or so later in the hospital
as he lies stunned by the failure of his heart
or lung. "Your father" is what she calls him,

wearing her permanent expression
of sadness, and the daughter, obese
and starved herself, calls him "Daddy,"
a child's word, crying for the tenderness
the two of them never knew. Nearby, her husband,
who resembles his father-in-law in spite
of his Elvis sideburns, doesn't say
even to himself what's going on inside him,
only grunts and stares as if the conversation
they were having concerned a missing bolt
or some extra job the higher-ups just gave him
because this is what you do if you're bound,
after an interminable, short life to be an old guy.

ANN MCNEAL

Walking Out

From bolted wooden desks
to electron-etched screens,
fifty-five years in school.
Early lessons well-learned—
Color between the lines.
Dead white men are
the poets. You'll be good
at science, it doesn't need
much imagination.
In my turn to teach, I schemed
to bring students power and joy,
danced molecules, embraced laughter.
Loving my work, I drop it now
on the floor like a still-warm
shirt, walk out the kitchen door
into the goldenrod meadow
already humming with bees.
The doe was here last night—
see the hollow where she slept.

ROBIN O. METZ

Father of the Bride

It is the cloudy morning
of my daughter's wedding,
and the men have gathered
in the gloom to play:
the groom, his father,
their rambunctious tribe—
footballers all.

We huddle;
the pass I throw
is rooted in an instinct
deeper than muscle or bone,
sinew or synapse, the stutter-
step of memory or the flicker of desire.
At this late hour, it is all I have to offer.

If truth be told,
there never was a plan:
receivers gulped a breath
and scurried; hopes were flung
in fits and starts with such impromptitude
and ardor as to seem outlandish some days,
or inspired, but every generation learns to scramble.

Now the spiral tightens,
climbs its arc and gains the apogee
beyond regret, beyond advice and pride,
beyond long rows, shortcuts, and pathways taken or deferred,
beyond my helping hands, however willing or well-meant,
for other hands, outstretched, are waiting, confidently poised . . .
and all is gathered in.

Who gives this child?
Your Honor, Holiness . . . I.
The sidelines blur before my eyes . . .
Attaboy! Have a seat ol' man!
I clap myself upon the back,
I pull the woolen cape about me.
Yes!

Deadwood

We pass in the hall with a cordial nod.
In afterthought, he turns and asks,
"What are you doing, now you're retired?"

His spontaneity catches me short:
He's over 70, been teaching almost 40 years,
professing his obsolescence through a one-way pipe
to minds examined like sponges
for their ability to absorb his reservoir of fact.

I dislike this man, and make my reply
overly enthusiastic: a bountiful list
he doesn't wish to hear.

He parries with complaints about his audience:
their decline in preparation,
sloppy dress, the admission standards gone awry.

I spy his yellowed notes peeking from a folder
he clutches to his chest. He says he can't retire:
wouldn't know what to do.

RICHARD MOORE

On Coming to Nothing

Old friends, nearing senility,
we sit, every last prospect dim,
and think: The world was wrong about me . . .
but at least it was right about him.

The Crossing

The snail at the edge of the road
inches forward, a trim gray finger
of a fellow in pinstripe suit.
He's burdened by his house
that has to follow
where he goes. Every inch,
he pulls together
all he is,
all he owns,
all he was given.

The road is wide
but he is called
by something
that knows him
on the other side.

EDITH NASH

Marriage

Before we were married
I always had a poached egg
on rye toast for breakfast
But since my husband
didn't like rye toast
And didn't want to eat
the same thing every day
I would make white toast,
and scramble or fry . . .

But I still liked eggs my way
So every once in a while
jaw set, lips clenched
I made rye toast for us both

And one day
Only 52 years later—
my husband looked at me and said,
"You know, rye toast and poached eggs
Are quite good."

NGUYEN BINH KHIEM

Retirement

translated by Nguyen Ngoc Bich

I'm more than seventy-four, and lucky
to be here at home, New Year—marvelous
to see the world reborn, though my house is poor
in all but books. Spring gardens, bamboos
blooming, house empty but for one
long clean chair, one bright window.
Who's right? Who's wrong? Who cares?
I only laugh at my own simple-mindedness.

Open House

I work as hard as I can
to have nothing to do.

Birds climb their rich ladder
of choruses.

They have tasted the top of the tree,
but they are not staying.

The whole sky says,
Your move.

ED OCHESTER

Anna Bachtle

Of course she's happy
in the kitchen
whose stone and metal
have been worn out by her flesh.
She's smoothed the clean linen
for fifty years;
in fall she laughs like a slice of moon
as she peels warm apples
into the battered colander in the sink.
The heavy cloth, the scent of fruit,
are comfortable things.
She is no appendix to her daughter's world.

Unless you escape in time,
she reviews forever the ancient pennants
on boats vanished from the river,
her first man's name,
the umbrella trees she saw one time in Kingston.
Seemingly content with chores,
with trees beyond the window
spinning familiar cycles,
she unfurls the wash like banners.
Surely her work is useful.
She earns her keep.
She tells her daughter's world as it runs
straight tracks toward its future,
"I am useful,
I am still here."

ALICIA OSTRIKER

Fifty

This is what a fifty-
Year-old woman looks like,
Said the glamorous feminist
Journalist when they asked her
How it felt to look so young.
A good answer.
But she didn't say, and they didn't
Ask her:
Did you expect the thread
Of your rough childhood
To unwind so far
From its beginnings?
Do you perhaps wonder,
When you try to look backward
And the thread seems invisible, as if
It has been snipped, who
In the world you are,
Stranger?
Do you think: *Let's keep this thing*
Rolling, keep on fighting, keep
Up the good work,
And glare down the steel tracks of the mirror
At the approach of the enemy
Who is still miles away
But coming like a commuter train, do you
Hit your typewriter
Every day, harder
And harder, like a recalcitrant
Spoiled child, have you surrendered
The hope of the perfect
Romance, or do you grip that
Fantasy stubbornly, like a kid holding

On to a dead pet
That she knows is dead

And do you make a joke of all of this
And when the clock says *Almost*
Quitting time, do you still answer *Never?*

GRACE PALEY

Here

Here I am in the garden laughing
an old woman with heavy breasts
and a nicely mapped face

how did this happen
well that's who I wanted to be

at last   a woman
in the old style   sitting
stout thighs apart under
a big skirt   grandchild sliding
on   off my lap   a pleasant
summer perspiration

that's my old man across the yard
he's talking to the meter reader
he's telling him the world's sad story
how electricity is oil or uranium
and so forth   I tell my grandson
run over to your grandpa   ask him
to sit beside me for a minute   I
am suddenly exhausted by my desire
to kiss his sweet explaining lips

REBECCA PARFITT 🖎

After the Ultrasound
for my grandchild

All night it rained softly
  all night the seals pop their shiny heads
  up out of the water and look softly
   at me
  We lean over the boat railing
  Look, seals! The children swimming!
   Look!

I will bring you to the water
I will sing you songs of nonsense & longing
  We will walk the cliffs
   naming the flowers as we go

   darling minnow
  deep sea explorer
jutting knee of you
tiny throbbing heart of you
pebble knobs of spine of you
  fingers fluttering toward your mouth
(just wait until you taste peaches)
  pinpoint toes oh my little seal
   the wonder of it!

Drawing for Absolute Beginners

Why was I there in that museum basement,
my arm and leg asleep in their cramped positions?
I would never draw the oval, nab the shadow, find the texture.
What could I do to soothe my frenzy of inability?
My clever classmates all got busy
while my muse turned into a schoolmarm. "Now, look,
there's a brown egg the shape of a plum.
It's the simplest shape in the world. It *begs* to be drawn!"
But when I looked down I saw
ten thousand miles to simplicity
and shivered.

      I thought of Bartleby. I preferred not to.
I shoved my muse into his sweater and we fled
into below-zero weather, drove to our apartment complex
where the orchids I'd wanted to draw
lolled above the frozen city, complex
and mystifying. "What's next?" my muse said,
after he had his tea and a cookie.
"I can barely follow them with my eye,
let alone with my pencil."
Let us try.

Retired

And so they ask: Jim,
whatta you do with all that time
now that you've quit the business?
Watch a lot of porno? TV and Twinkies?
Sleep in? What's a bald guy of 58,
still healthy and wise, do with himself
when his wife goes off to work
at 7 AM and the day just beginning?
And when Jim says no to all
of the above and says instead
a little of this, a little of that,
and they grin and say, no, really,
what the hell you do with yourself
all day long, he finally gives in
and says something juicy
like there are these two widow
women in the neighborhood
who twice a week at ten come by
to share the art of meditation
over medication, after which
he serves a stimulating tea
and something sweet like banana
nut bread made teasingly moist
with slices of fresh pear gently folded in
only moments before filling
the greased pan and slipping it in
the oven, if you know what I mean,
Jim says, and they, thinking they do,
nod and grin like schoolboys.

RONALD PIES

The Neurology Professor Retires

Died Without Issue.
  Decessit sine prole,
if you like a gravedigger's Latin.
  Well, I've been childless in the flesh
these fifty semesters,
  but have fathered rich earth
in you, my bean-pole brood,
  my classroom seedlings.
Died without issue?
  "Raise up many disciples"
the Talmud says,
  and if smart-asses count,
I've done that—watched you walk
  white-coated
into the blighted world
  with tricks I taught you,
words I thought wise—
  and how to tell Kernig's
from Brudzinski's sign.
  Died without issue?
My God, I've propagated
  like an over-ripe seed-pod
torn apart—and sent the world
  a thousand children
armed with reflex hammers
  and soldier's heart.

The Cold

I can't remember what I was thinking . . . the cold
Outside numbs purposes to a blur, and people
Seem to be more explicitly animal—

Stamping the snow, our visible patient breath
Around our faces. When we come inside
An air of mortal health steams up from our coats,

Blood throbbing richer in the whitest faces.
When I stop working, I feel it in a draft
Leaking in somewhere. In the hardware store—

I think because it was a time of day
When people mostly are at work—it seemed
All of the other customers were old,

A group I think of five or six . . . a vague
Memory of white hair or of elder voices,
Their heavy protective coats and gloves and boots

Holding the creature warmth around their bodies.
I think that someone talked about the weather;
It was gray, then; then brighter after noon

For an hour or two. As if half-senile already,
In a winter blank, I had the stupid thought
About old age as cozy—drugged convalescence;

A forgetful hardihood of naps and drinks;
Peaceful, without the fears, pains, operations
That make life bitterest, one hears, near the end . . .

The needle *Work* unthreaded—not misplaced.
Bitterest at its own close, the short harsh day
Does lead us to hover an extra minute or two

Inside our lighted offices and stores
With our coats buttoned, holding the keys perhaps;
Or like me, working in a room, alone,

Watching out from a window, where the wind
Lifts up the snow from loaded roofs and branches,
A cold pale smoke against the sky's darkening gray—

Watching it now, not having been out in hours,
I come up closer idly, to feel the cold,
Forgetting for a minute what I was doing.

Comfort Zone

Who meant to stay here this long? Anywhere. This job. This
comfort zone as my colleague calls it. Tells me she's growing
her hair a bit to get out of her comfort zone. *Fleur de lis.*
Montezuma sounding on the computer-generated carillon,

its loudspeaker perched on top of the concrete bunker
of building C, and the woman yesterday opening the bathroom door
with her hands carefully gloved in brown paper towels.
Who thought we could live this long? Get this worried. Be this

stupid. Go square like this. I meant to stay out of it. Janis
downstairs 30 years after her death begging some bad boy
to take another piece of her heart, and sort of buzzed, I go down,
I dance and shout with her. *You know you got it, if it makes*

you feel good I sing word for word, the dance steps
perfect if you can call my kind of dancing, dancing.

Letter of Transmittal

Herein find one woman, used, in fair shape,
given to excess, too fond of what's personal
to star in meetings, intuitive
rather than learned as we say,
whose favorite pastime is the job
you've offered (which in our service
she defined), whose greatest accomplishment
is drawing breath.

On the office phone we heard
she heard this counsel, part of her job,
to pet the scar, croon to her body,
the surviving parts, sway and cherish
like a lover all that falls easily
into the upturned palm. Representative
of the job she's done.

Her last assignment is her signature, here
at the bottom of this letter. Take her.
We have voted, given voice to her eulogy.
Where she goes now is her own affair.
Our names are below. Take her.
Everything we have been able to do
for her is done. What's left is truly bone.
If you wish it, take her home.

The South Berkeley Branch Closes

They closed down the branch
That served black neighborhoods
Now, the elderly from the
Harriet Tubman Homes and the
Sojourner Truth Manor
Have to taxi to
The middle aged
Urban professionals'
Branch
It will take extra pains for
Them to make deposits and withdrawals
Located near latte cafes
And ice cream parlors
Boutiques, art cinemas
Gourmet supermarkets
And salons
You can get your legs waxed
There for forty dollars
There will be even longer
Delays when I cash my check
They will make phone calls to
See whether I am whom I say
I am
The bank manager will look
Up at me as the clerk shows
Her my signature
The bank guard will glare at me
I have been their customer
For over 25 years
I won't go anywhere near
Their new location
I stick out like a sore
Thumb in this neighborhood

Plain-clothes men will follow me
Wherever I go and
Video cameras
VHS my every move
Pale pale women will dog my path
Traveling from my house
To this part of town
Will become a Freedom Ride

FRANCINE RINGOLD

Luke Like Life
Central Park, July 14, 2001

Luke, with the plump legs,
is a flirt, songs flying as he is
bounced on the knees of the West Indian
with sugar on her lips. Surely,
this is how it must feel to ride the wild bears
that hide in the park, as the bears smile,
their gaze distant as the trees they once climbed.

And in the stifling apartment above,
a man closes his eyes on the light and sleeps.

Know that I love you there
in the cell of your intention;
that I have gone to the children,
to Luke and Laura of the shining black eyes
and Sarah, sure in each plunge into the unknown,
to greet you, to say, just once,
it is all right. Laura whispers in unison
with the wind, arms outstretched to catch
some hint of direction, then struggles with Rosa,
feet planted to hold her place,
as the fierce one pulls the sand
from beneath her feet, that sand

always shifting, just as we try to dig our feet
more firmly into the earth, sloughing off
each day as the tide washes in and out
and we watch unable to hold our place,
comforted only by the hymn of the waves,
the crisp clacking of the gulls, the slight hint
that even as our prints slide out to sea
there are the children of our mind,
the daughters of our body, the hands
that hold each bony finger,
thankful for the ride we share.

The Conversation of Old Husbands

She's gone, Clemente, I know.
But I see her in your eyes,
I see what you're looking at
When you look away.
Where your eyes used to be
I see her.
Where you once had a tongue
You now wear a bow-tie.
Old man, I understand.
I remember when you told me
You saw her neck
And when you did
It was as if she were outlined
And not a part of the world,
Like a photograph
Lying on a newspaper,
Just there at that moment,
Bigger than the moment.
I thought of the dotted lines
They used to put around paper dolls
But it wasn't dashes around her,
They were sparks.
Still, it was as if she were cut out
From the world
Anyway, something saved
Off the page. It's something you told me
And which I've remembered,
Exactly as you said it.
Wherever she is
When you look at her, Clemente,
I see her too.

Report from the Stratosphere

Travel ahead, reads my horoscope.
A frequent flyer with no boarding pass,
airsick on rougher flights,
I finger the warty globe, hesitate.

Travel ahead. Verb or noun? Safer than
backward travel, paddling into the past
in my leaky canoe, or tacking my iceboat
against the wind over a crumpled pond.

Travel ahead, always ahead, instructions
cackle from the socked-in control tower.
Ignoring iced wings, weather reports, war zones,
at last I taxi into the blizzard

punching buttons, spinning knobs,
clutching the stick, clutching the clutch,
clutching whatever might weigh me down—
Scattering maps, I soar beyond orbit.

CLAUDETTE MORK SIGG

Barre Exercises

I watch myself as I dance, dissect each move I make,
but it's not me I see, the old woman with creaking joints,
cartilage worn away in both knees, straining Achilles,
but the way I once was, schoolgirl with pale skin,
long-legged, tiny-waisted, breathless and nearly breastless,
gliding down to the floor in a *plié*, heels coming up,
knees out. Left arm unfolds, pale gold in the thin streak
of sunlight staining the worn floor with amber.

The mirror wavers, distorts as I move from one
reflection to the next, the woman as I am now, not
the girl with leg half outstretched, frozen, head turned
to one side, listening to a spasm, a betrayal of muscles
creeping down the calf, tweaking the arch. I massage my knee,
the touch of Mr. B.'s cane on my thigh the faintest
of memories, discarded with toe shoes and lamb's wool—
but the girl, bone-marrow deep, insistent, clamorous,
still dances her invisible waltz across my interior floors.

You Reading This, Be Ready

Starting here, what do you want to remember?
How sunlight creeps along a shining floor?
What scent of old wood hovers, what softened
sound from outside fills the air?

Will you ever bring a better gift for the world
than the breathing respect that you carry
wherever you go right now? Are you waiting
for time to show you some better thoughts?

When you turn around, starting here, lift this
new glimpse that you found; carry into evening
all that you want from this day. This interval you spent
reading or hearing this, keep it for life—

What can anyone give you greater than now,
starting here, right in this room, when you turn around?

GERALD STERN ~~

This Was a Wonderful Night

This was a wonderful night. I heard the Brahms
piano quintet, I read a poem by Schiller,
I read a story, I listened to *Gloomy Sunday*.
No one called me, I studied the birthday poem
of Alvaro de Campos. I thought, if there was time,
I'd think of my garden—all that lettuce, wasted,
all those huge tomatoes lying on the ground
rotting, and I'd think of the sticks I put there,
waving good-bye, those bearded sticks. De Campos,
he was the one who suffered most, his birthday
was like a knife to him; he sat in a chair
remembering his aunts; he thought of the flowers
and cakes, he thought of the sideboard crowded with gifts.
I look at the photo of Billie Holiday;
I turn the lightbulb on and off. I envy
those poets who loved their childhood, those who remember
the extra places laid out, the china and glasses.
They want to devour the past, they revel in pity,
they live like burnt-out matches, memory ruins them;
again and again they go back to the first place.

De Campos and I are sitting on a bench
in some American city. He hardly knows
how much I love his country. I have two things
to tell him about my childhood, one is the ice
on top of the milk, one is the sign in the window—
three things—the smell of coal. There is some snow
left on the street, the wind is blowing. He trembles
and touches the buttons on his vest. His house
is gone, his aunts are dead, the tears run down
our cheeks and chins, we are like babies, crying.
"Leave thinking to the head," he says. I sob,
"I don't have birthdays any more," I say,

"I just go on," although I hardly feel
the sadness, there is such joy in being there
on that small bench, watching the sycamores,
looking for birds in the snow, listening for boots,
staring at the begonias, getting up
and down to rub the leaves and touch the buds—
endless pleasure, talking about New York,
comparing pain, writing the names down
of all the cities south of Lisbon, singing
one or two songs—a hundred years for him,
a little less for me, going east and west
in the new country, my heart forever pounding.

Now I'm Retired, I Have Time

to dig up the front yard burdock;
fork under the dandelion sod;
work out on weight machines
when no one's at the gym;
bike through burnished prairie
before frost kills the goldenrod;

change into my robe at noon
and sit at the dining room table,
waiting for words to come;
nap with the cat on the sofa
when we find a spot of sun;

read *War and Peace*; take up
the cello; clean up the study;
donate the dot-matrix printer
to St. Vincent de Paul;

put old snaphots in albums;
create an e-mail address book;
spend all day on the Internet;

sleep late on a fall-dark morning
ignoring the phone and dreaming

old lovers, illness, death.

BRUCE TAYLOR

Wednesday, the Hole

Isn't often you see a hole dug
as deep as this one up here so
when the county came to dig it
most of the old men came around
sometime during the day to watch.

So there were usually four
or five guys standing around
watching three guys standing around
watching one guy dig, and the boss
came by twice to check, and the Power
& Light guys stopped by too.

And the kids on their trikes,
painted red white & blue,
were warned "don't get too close"
but did and it was all too much
for Happy, Ray's penned-up
husky pup, who's learned to ignore
the tomcat's strut or another
fat rabbit fattening upon
clover in the patchy lawn.

Lunchtime, the crew took their pails
to the shady side of the truck
and someone brought ice-tea
and Ray smuggled them a beer each.
Then it was back to work so
a different guy dug and Ray took
the Buick to the Super-A
for popsicles and more beer.

MARILYN L. TAYLOR

Aunt Eudora's Harlequin Romance

She turns the bedlamp on. The book falls open
in her mottled hands, and while she reads
her mouth begins to quiver, forming words
like *Breathless. Promises. Elope.*
As she turns the leaves, Eudora's cheek
takes on a bit of bloom. Her frowzy hair
thickens and turns gold, her dim eyes clear,
the wattles vanish from her slender neck.
Her waist, emerging from its ring of flesh,
bends to the side. Breasts that used to hang
like pockets rise and ripen; her long legs
tremble. Her eyes close, she holds her breath—
the steamy pages flutter by, unread,
as lover after lover finds her bed.

A Three-Year-Old Visits

We saunter over to the tomato vines—
bracketed by thin poles—and I advise
"Just pick the ripe ones."
What does "ripe" mean, you ask?

In my lengthening shadow
I want to define it as:
nodding to the future,

mature, bold, mellow,
like apples edging toward cider,
like the ruby grape ready for pressing.

But I say, "Ripe means perfect,
sweet, red, ready, just right,
like the age of three; like you
visiting me in my garden."

RONALD WALLACE

Blessings

occur.
Some days I find myself
putting my foot in
the same stream twice;
leading a horse to water
and making him drink.
I have a clue.
I can see the forest
for the trees.

All around me people
are making silk purses
out of sows' ears,
getting blood from turnips,
building Rome in a day.
There's a business
like show business.
There's something new
under the sun.

Some days misery
no longer loves company;
it puts itself out of its.
There's rest for the weary.
There's turning back.
There are guarantees.
I can be serious.
I can mean that.
You can quite
put your finger on it.

Some days I know
I am long for this world.

I can go home again.
And when I go
I can
take it with me.

Contributors

DOUG ANDERSON has written three books of poems, as well as fiction, drama, and filmscripts. He is at work on a memoir about the Vietnam War in the 1960s. He teaches at the University of Connecticut.

WERNER ASPENSTRÖM (1918–1997) grew up in rural Dalarna, Sweden, but spent his adult life in Stockholm. His poems and essays made him a highly respected and much loved figure in current Swedish literature. He was a member of the Swedish Academy.

JOHN BALABAN is the author of twelve books of poetry and prose, including, most recently, *Path, Crooked Path*. *Locusts at the Edge of Summer: New and Selected Poems* was a finalist for the National Book Award and a winner of the William Carlos Williams Award.

MEG BARDEN is an eighty-six-year-old retired college professor enjoying life in Keene, New Hampshire, where she serves on the board of directors of Monadnock Writers' Group. She recently edited their fifth anthology, *Private Places*, in which she has a story.

ELINOR BENEDICT is a former teacher, journalist, and editor living in the Upper Peninsula of Michigan. Her collection *All That Divides Us* won the 2000 May Swenson Poetry Award from Utah State University Press.

GEORGE BILGERE's most recent collection of poems is *The Good Kiss*. His poems have appeared in *Poetry, Ploughshares, The Georgia Review, Shenandoah*, and elsewhere. He is a 2002 recipient of a Witter Bynner Fellowship from the Library of Congress.

CHANA BLOCH is the author of three books of poems, *The Secrets of the Tribe, The Past Keeps Changing*, and the award-winning *Mrs. Dumpty*. She is cotranslator of the biblical *Song of Songs*, as well as books by Israeli poets Dahlia Ravikovitch and Yehuda Amichai.

PHILIP BOOTH has published numerous books of poetry, including *Lifelines: Selected Poems, 1950–1999* (1999), *Pairs* (1994), and the children's book *Crossing* (2001). Honors include Guggenheim, Rockefeller, and National Endowment for the Arts fellowships.

JONATHAN BRACKER's poems have appeared in *America, Poetry Northwest,* the *New Yorker,* and *Southern Poetry Review,* among others. He is the author of three chapbooks and editor of *Bright Cages: The Selected Poems of Christopher Morley.*

JOHN BRANDI, poet and painter, lives in northern New Mexico. Recent books include *Reflections in the Lizard's Eye* (prose), *In What Disappears* (poetry), and three haiku collections: *Empty Moon Belly Full, One Cup and Another,* and *Weeding the Cosmos.*

BILL BROWN is the author of four collections of poetry, including *The Gods of Little Pleasures.* His work has appeared recently in *Southern Poetry Review, Rhino, Terminus, Appalachian Heritage,* and *Smartish Pace,* among others.

CHARLES CANTRELL's poems have appeared in numerous journals, including the *Literary Review, Poetry Northwest,* and *Prairie Schooner.* His chapbooks are *Cicatrix* and *Greatest Hits.* He teaches English at Madison Area Technical College in Wisconsin.

HAYDEN CARRUTH, author of thirty-one books including, most recently, *Doctor Jazz* (2002), is a recipient of numerous awards, including the National Book Critics Circle Award for *Collected Shorter Poems, 1946–1991,* and the National Book Award for *Scrambled Eggs and Whiskey* (1996).

GRACE CAVALIERI is the author of fourteen books of poetry, twenty produced plays, and texts of two operas. She has produced "The Poet and the Poem" on public radio, now broadcast from the Library of Congress via NPR satellite. She holds the Allen Ginsberg Award for Poetry.

THOMAS CENTOLELLA's most recent book is *Views from along the Middle Way.* He has been the recipient of the Lannon Literary Fellowship, the American Book Award, and the California Book Award. He works part-time for San Francisco's Institute on Aging.

ROBIN CHAPMAN's most recent collections include *The Way In* and, with coauthor J. C. Sprott, *Images of a Complex World: The Art and Poetry of Chaos.* Her poems have appeared in the *American Scholar,* the *Hudson Review,* and *Poetry.*

KELLY CHERRY is the author of over twenty books, including

History, Passion, Freedom, Death, and Hope: Prose about Poetry
and the novels *We Can Still Be Friends* and *In the Wink of an Eye*.
She lives with her husband on a small farm in Southside, Virginia.

LUCILLE CLIFTON's twelve collections include *Mercy* (2004),
Blessing the Boats (2002), which won the National Book Award,
and *The Terrible Stories* (1995). In 1999 she was elected a
chancellor of The Academy of American Poets.

STEPHANIE KAPLAN COHEN's poetry has appeared in the *New York
Times, Spillway, Confluence,* and *Iconoclast*. She is also a short
story writer and columnist: "Ask Stephanie" appears in the
Alzheimer's Association Quarterly in Westchester and Putnam,
New York.

RUTH DAIGON was founder and editor of the poetry magazine *Poets
On:* and has published seven collections. Her poetry awards include
the Ann Stanford Poetry Prize and the Greensboro Poetry Award.

MARTHA L. DEED lives near the mouth of the Erie Canal in North
Tonawanda, New York. Recent work has appeared in *Iowa Review
Web, Gypsy, Shampoo, Moria, Milk, Big Bridge,* and other print
and online journals.

MARCIA DENIUS teaches writing courses at the Florida Institute of
Technology in Melbourne, Florida.

MARY L. DOWNS writes in Appleton, Wisconsin. Her work has
appeared in *Wisconsin Academy Review,* the *Scene,* the *Lyric,
C/Q, Wisconsin Poets' Calendar,* and other publications.

STEPHEN DUNN is the author of thirteen collections of poetry,
including *Different Hours,* which was awarded the 2001 Pulitzer
Prize.

SUSAN ELBE is the author of *Light Made from Nothing*. Her poems
have appeared in many journals, including *CALYX, Comstock
Review, MARGIE, North American Review, Passages North,* and
Smartish Pace.

R. VIRGIL "RON" ELLIS is associate editor of *Rosebud* magazine.
His poems have appeared in *Poetry Northwest, Mississippi
Review, Switched-on Gutenberg,* and many others. His latest
release as a performance poet is the CD entitled *The Andro Poems:
A Rock Cantata.*

DIANE GLANCY retired from Macalester College after seventeen
years teaching Native American literature and creative writing.

Her most recent works include *The Dance Partner: Stories of the Ghost Dance*, *Rooms: New and Selected Poems*, and the play *Stone Heart*.

SAM HAMILL is a poet and translator who has published more than forty books, most recently *Almost Paradise: New and Selected Poems and Translations* and a translation of the Tao Te Ching. He is the director of Poets Against War and for thirty-two years was editor at Copper Canyon Press.

JIM HANLEN retired from teaching in Kelso, Washington, to live in Anchorage, Alaska, close by the Chugach Mountains.

ALBERT HUFFSTICKLER (1927–2002) of Austin, Texas, was the author of *Walking Wounded*, *The Wander Years*, and the forthcoming *Just So Nobody Feels Left Out: Poems by Albert Huffstickler*.

BENJAMIN HUSTED, retired professor of music theory and composition from Mansfield University in Pennsylvania, began writing poetry at age eighty-two.

MARK IRWIN is the author of five collections of poetry, including *White City* (2000), nominated for the National Book Critics Circle Award, and *Bright Hunger*. Recipient of the James Wright Poetry Award, he divides his time between Colorado and Los Angeles.

RUTH HARRIET JACOBS is the author of nine books, including *Be an Outrageous Older Woman*. The retired chair of sociology at Clark University, her poems have appeared in many journals and anthologies.

JESSE LEE KERCHEVAL is the author of seven books of fiction, nonfiction, and poetry, including the collections *Dog Angel* and *World as Dictionary* and the chapbook *Chartreuse*.

CAROLYN KIZER is eighty-two. She has written eight books of poetry and a chapbook, *Pro Femina*. Her book *Yin* won the Pulitzer Prize in 1985.

KLIPSCHUTZ is the pen name of Kurt Lipschutz of San Francisco. He is the author of three collections of poetry, including *The Good Neighbor Policy* (1989) and *Twilight of the Male Ego* (2002).

TED KOOSER is a recent U.S. Poet Laureate and the winner of the 2005 Pulitzer Prize for Poetry. He is a retired life insurance executive who lives in rural Nebraska.

ELLEN KORT has authored thirteen books and served as Wisconsin's first Poet Laureate (2000–2004). She travels nationally and internationally presenting readings, poetry workshops, and creative writing residencies.

MAXINE KUMIN's fifteenth poetry collection is *Jack and Other New Poems*. Her awards include the Ruth E. Lilly Poetry Prize and the Pulitzer Prize. She served as Consultant in Poetry to the Library of Congress in 1980–81. She and her husband live on a farm in New Hampshire.

DENISE LEVERTOV (1923–1997) published over twenty volumes of poetry, including the posthumous *This Great Unknowing: Last Poems* (1999).

SANDRA LINDOW has published four poetry chapbooks and won the 1989 Posner Award and the 2003 Wisconsin Press Women's Award for poetry. For over twenty years she has worked as a reading specialist in a treatment center for emotionally disturbed adolescents.

ARLENE L. MANDELL's previous careers include writer for *Good Housekeeping* magazine, public relations executive, and English teacher. In the past fifteen years, her work has appeared in more than two hundred literary journals and seven anthologies.

LENORE MAYHEW lives in Oberlin, Ohio. She is the translator of *Poem Without a Hero and Other Poems* by Anna Akhmatova. Her own poems have appeared in *Field* and *Atlanta Review*, among other journals.

JERI MCCORMICK is the recipient of a Wisconsin Arts Board Fellowship and an Outstanding Achievement Award from the Wisconsin Library Association. Her book, *When It Came Time*, was published in Ireland.

WESLEY MCNAIR is the author of eight collections of poetry, including *The Ghosts of You & Me* (2006). He is currently Professor Emeritus and Writer in Residence at the University of Maine at Farmington.

ANN MCNEAL lives and roams the hills near Amherst, Massachusetts. She taught biology at Hampshire College for more than thirty years and has now retired to write. Her poems have appeared in *A Moving Journal, Earth's Daughters, Patchwork Journal*, and *White Heron*, among others.

ROBIN O. METZ directs the program in creative writing at Knox College. His collection *Unbidden Angel* received the Rainer Maria

Rilke International Poetry Prize. His work has appeared in the *Paris Review, International Poetry Review,* and *Epoch,* among other journals.

JOHNES K. MOORE is a retired professor of marine science from Salem State College, Massachusetts. Having taught oceanography and ecology for twenty-five years, he now writes poetry in retirement.

RICHARD MOORE has published a novel, translations of plays by Plautus and Euripides, a book of essays on poetry, and ten books of his own poetry. He taught poetry at the New England Conservatory of Music before he retired.

RUTH MOOSE is the author of two collections of short stories and four collections of poetry, including *Smith Grove.* She is a lecturer in the creative writing program at the University of North Carolina–Chapel Hill.

EDITH NASH (1913–2003) was a political activist who helped end school segregation in Washington, D.C., and author of *Practice the Here and Now: Selected Writings of Edith Nash* (2001).

NGUYEN BINH KHIEM (1491–1585) was a Vietnamese courtier, scholar, and poet, but he is even better known as a seer—on the level of Nostradamus. The product of a parlous era, he chose to retire early to a simple life of communion with nature and books.

NAOMI SHIHAB NYE's most recent books are *A Maze Me: Poems for Girls, Going Going* (a novel), and the poetry collection *You and Yours.* She and her husband, the photographer Michael Nye, have lived for a quarter of a century in old downtown San Antonio.

ED OCHESTER's most recent books are *Snow White Horses: Selected Poems* and *The Land of Cockaigne.* He edits the Pitt Poetry Series and, with Judith Vollmer, the poetry magazine *5 AM;* he teaches in the MFA program at Bennington College.

ALICIA OSTRIKER's eleven collections of poetry include *No Heaven; The Imaginary Lover,* winner of the William Carlos Williams Award; and *The Crack in Everything* and *The Little Space: Poems Selected and New,* both National Book Award finalists.

GRACE PALEY is a political activist, short-story writer, and poet who lives in Vermont. *Begin Again: Collected Poems* is her most recent collection.

REBECCA PARFITT is the author of *The Birth Primer* and numerous poems, some published. She works as a domestic violence counselor in DeKalb, Illinois.

MOLLY PEACOCK is the author of five volumes of poetry, including *Cornucopia: New & Selected Poems*. Her poems have appeared in the *New Yorker*, the *Nation*, the *New Republic*, the *Paris Review*, as well as the *Best of the Best American Poetry*.

ROGER PFINGSTON is a retired teacher. He's the author of *Singing to the Garden* and *Earthbound*. His work has appeared recently in *Poetry East* and *Quarterly West*.

RONALD PIES, M.D., teaches at both Tufts and Harvard medical schools. He has published poetry in many literary magazines and anthologies, and in his collection *Creeping Thyme*.

ROBERT PINSKY is the author of many books of poetry, including *Jersey Rain* and *The Figured Wheel*, and of the award-winning translation *The Inferno of Dante*. His prose works include *The Situation of Poetry* and *The Sounds of Poetry*.

CAROL POTTER's third book of poems, *Short History of Pets*, won the 1999 Cleveland State Poetry Center Award and the Valcones Award. Her poems have appeared in *Field*, the *Iowa Review*, *Poetry*, and other journals.

HILDA RAZ is the author of *Trans* and *Divine Honors*, among many other books, and is the editor of *Prairie Schooner*.

ISHMAEL REED, author of over twenty books, is a poet, novelist, playwright, and essayist. Recent collections include *The Reed Reader*, *Another Day at the Front*, and *Blues City: A Walk in Oakland*. Collaborations with musicians have resulted in the CDs *Conjure I, II, & III*.

FRANCINE RINGOLD is the poet laureate of Oklahoma and the editor of *Nimrod*. Her most recent poetry collections include *The Trouble with Voices*, winner of the Oklahoma Book Award, and *Every Other One*, a collaboration with her husband, poet Manly Johnson.

ALBERTO RÍOS's eight collections of poetry include *The Smallest Muscle in the Human Body*, a finalist for the National Book Award, and *The Theater of Night*. He has also written short stories and a memoir, *Capirotada*, about growing up on the Mexican border.

ELISAVIETTA RITCHIE is the author of *In Haste I Write You This Note: Stories & Half-Stories*, winner of the Washington Writers'

Fiction Competition. Her poetry includes *The Arc of the Storm* and *Elegy for the Other Woman: New & Selected Terribly Female Poems.*

CLAUDETTE MORK SIGG taught in a ghetto high school for thirty years and now volunteers as a docent at the Oakland Museum, California. Her poetry has appeared in *Atlanta Review* and other journals and anthologies.

WILLIAM STAFFORD (1914–1993) was the author of over fifty books and recipient of the National Book Award for *Traveling through the Dark.* After serving as Consultant in Poetry to the Library of Congress in 1970, he was named Oregon's poet laureate in 1975.

GERALD STERN's most recent book of poems is *Everything Is Burning.* He is the 2005 winner of the Wallace Stevens Prize from the Academy of American Poetry. He retired in 1996.

JUDITH STRASSER is the author of the memoir *Black Eye: Escaping a Marriage, Writing a Life* and two poetry collections, *Sand Island Succession* and *The Reason/Unreason Project,* which won the Lewis-Clark Press Expedition Award.

BRUCE TAYLOR's poetry has appeared in the *Chicago Review,* the *Nation,* the *New York Quarterly,* and *Poetry.* His most recent book is *Pity the World: Poems Selected and New.*

MARILYN L. TAYLOR was poet laureate of Milwaukee for 2004–2005. Recent work has appeared in *Poetry,* the *American Scholar, Iris,* and the *Formalist.* She teaches at the University of Wisconsin-Milwaukee, Woodland Pattern Book Center, and elsewhere.

DONNA WAHLERT is the author of *The First Pressing: Poetry of the Everyday.* Her work has been widely anthologized, most recently in *Proposing on the Brooklyn Bridge: Wedding Blessings* and *Bless the Beasts: Children's Prayers and Poems about Animals.*

RONALD WALLACE's twelve books of fiction, poetry, and criticism include *Long for This World: New and Selected Poems, The Uses of Adversity,* and *Quick Bright Things.* He is codirector of creative writing at the University of Wisconsin–Madison.

Acknowledgments

ANDERSON, DOUG. "Sixty-One" originally appeared in *Poetry*. Copyright © 2004 by Doug Anderson. Reprinted with permission of the author.

ASPENSTRÖM, WERNER. "Who Is Not a Child" originally appeared in the *Quarterly Review of Literature*. Copyright © 1996 by Robin Fulton. Translated from the Swedish by Robin Fulton. Reprinted with permission of Signe Lund-Aspenström and the translator.

BALABAN, JOHN. "Eliseo's Cabin, Taos Pueblo" from *Locusts at the Edge of Summer*. Copyright © 1997 by John Balaban. Reprinted with permission of Copper Canyon Press.

BARDEN, MEG. "Reaching Eighty." Copyright © 2005 by Meg Barden. Reprinted with permission of the author.

BENEDICT, ELINOR. "Bamboo" from *All That Divides Us*. Copyright © 2000 by Elinor Benedict. Reprinted with permission of Utah State University Press.

BILGERE, GEORGE. "Unwise Purchases" originally appeared in *Rattle*. Copyright © 2002 by George Bilgere. Reprinted with permission of the author.

BLOCH, CHANA. "The Sixth Age" originally appeared in the *Kenyon Review*. Copyright © 2005 by Chana Bloch. Reprinted with permission of the author.

BOOTH, PHILIP. "Pairs" from *Pairs* published by Viking-Penguin. Copyright © 1999 by Philip Booth. Reprinted with permission of the author.

BRACKER, JONATHAN. "Wait-Time Is Currently about Twelve Minutes." Copyright © 2005 by Jonathan Bracker. Reprinted with permission of the author.

BRANDI, JOHN. [thinking of retirement]. Copyright © 2005 by John Brandi. Reprinted with permission of the author.

BROWN, BILL. "Waking" originally appeared in *Into the Teeth of the Wind*. Copyright © 2000 by Bill Brown. Reprinted with permission of the author.

CANTRELL, CHARLES. "Retirement Matters." Copyright © 2005 by Charles Cantrell. Reprinted with permission of the author.

CARRUTH, HAYDEN. "At Seventy-Five: Rereading an Old Book" from *Doctor Jazz: Poems*. Copyright © 2001 by Hayden Carruth. Reprinted with permission of Copper Canyon Press.

CAVALIERI, GRACE. "In the Pinecrest Rest Home" from *Pinecrest Rest Haven* published by The Word Works. Copyright © 1998 by Grace Cavalieri. Reprinted with permission of the author.

CENTOLELLA, THOMAS. "Some Little Happiness" from *Views from along the Middle Way* published by Copper Canyon Press. Copyright © 2002 by Thomas Centolella. Reprinted with permission of the author.

KERCHEVAL, JESSE LEE. "Ham and the Moon" from *World as Dictionary*, published by Carnegie Mellon University Press. Copyright © 1999 by Jesse Lee Kercheval. Reprinted with permission of the author.

KIZER, CAROLYN. "Parents' Pantoum" from *Cool, Calm & Collected: Poems 1960–2000*. Copyright © 2001 by Carolyn Kizer. Reprinted with permission of Copper Canyon Press.

KLIPSCHUTZ. "Office" from *The Good Neighbor Policy*, published by End of the Century Press. Copyright © 1989 by Kurt Lipschutz. Reprinted with permission of the author.

KOOSER, TED. "Applesauce" from *Delights & Shadows*, published by Copper Canyon Press. Copyright © 2004 by Ted Kooser. Reprinted with permission of the author.

KORT, ELLEN. "One by One." Copyright © 2004 by Ellen Kort. Reprinted with permission of the author.

KUMIN, MAXINE. "Women and Horses" from *Jack and Other New Poems*. Copyright © 2005 by Maxine Kumin. Reprinted with permission of W. W. Norton & Company, Inc.

LEVERTOV, DENISE. "Living Alone (III)" from *The Freeing of the Dust*. Copyright © 1975 by Denise Levertov. Reprinted with permission of New Directions Publishing Corp.

LINDOW, SANDRA. "The Physicist's Warning" originally appeared in *Asimov's Science Fiction Magazine*. Copyright © 2005 by Sandra Lindow. Reprinted with permission of the author.

MANDELL, ARLENE L. "All Dressed Up." Copyright © 2004 by Arlene L. Mandell. Reprinted with permission of the author.

MAYHEW, LENORE. "Almost Eighty" originally appeared in *Field*. Copyright © 2003 by Lenore Mayhew. Reprinted with permission of Oberlin College Press.

MCCORMICK, JERI. "Bureaucrat Tells How" originally appeared in *Rosebud*. Copyright © 1996 by Jeri McCormick. Reprinted with permission of the author.

MCNAIR, WESLEY. "Old Guys" originally appeared in *Poetry Northwest*. Copyright © 1998 by Wesley McNair. Reprinted with permission of the author.

MCNEAL, ANN. "Walking Out." Copyright © 2004 by Ann McNeal. Reprinted with permission of the author.

METZ, ROBIN O. "Father of the Bride" originally appeared in the *Reply of the Tongues*. Copyright © 2006 by Robin Metz. Reprinted with permission of the author.

MOORE, JOHNES K. "Deadwood" originally appeared in *Sextant: The Journal of Salem State College*. Copyright © 1998 by Johnes K. Moore. Reprinted with permission of the author.

MOORE, RICHARD. "On Coming to Nothing" originally appeared in *Poetry*. Copyright © 1981 by Richard Moore. Reprinted with permission of the author.

Index to Titles